Poverty
in
Cambridgeshire

MICHAEL J. MURPHY

The Oleander Press
17 Stansgate Avenue
Cambridge CB2 2QZ

©1978 Michael Joseph Murphy and The Oleander Press

ISBN 0 900891 29 7

Acknowledgements

I wish to thank the staff of the Cambridgeshire Collection of Cambridge-shire Libraries, Cambridge University Library, and County Record Office. I owe a particular debt of gratitude to M. Moriarty B.A. (Oxon.) for his critical reading of the preliminary draft and his perceptive and valuable comments. Permission to reproduce illustrations was kindly given by the Shakespeare Birthplace Trust, Stratford-upon-Avon; the Wisbech and Fenland Museum; and the Cambridgeshire Collection, the County Record Office, and the Cambridge Antiquarian Society, Cambridge.

Front cover illustration: Illustration of the Whig Poor Laws. Barn Ill Workhouse, 1837.

Back cover illustration: Poor Law Notice, 1830s. [St. Andrew the Less].

Title page illustration: Gypsies, 1920s.

Designed by Ron Jones

Origination by Cambridgeshire Life Ltd, St. Ives, Cambs.

Printed and bound by Nicholson and Jermayne, Hertford, Herts.

❦1❦
Poverty in the Middle Ages

Poverty was endemic in medieval Cambridgeshire. The living standard of the mass of the people was low. Life on the margin of subsistence, at the mercy of plague, famine and war, was the common expectation of the peasant. In the face of such uncontrollable and destructive elements in social life, prayer and trust in God and His church often appeared the only recourse. Nevertheless, uncertain as times were, the pressures that beset many of the poor nowadays were absent from the medieval scene. At least the Church and richer members of society recognised it as their Christian duty to succour 'God's poor' and to care for the sick and needy. There was hunger and uncertainty, but no widespread fear of unemployment; sickness was not an economic calamity, nor was the advent of old age often overshadowed by the prospects of loneliness and privation. Organized in tight, closely-knit communities centring on manor, gild and church, medieval society evolved its own voluntary system to deal with the familiar, recurring insecurities that developed within it.

To the medieval Christian, poverty was part of the nature of things. Christ had been poor and the poor who suffered their lot patiently could expect their just reward in the next life. But life in this world could be brutally hard. Throughout the county the rural labouring poor lived in tent-shaped, dark, draughty, smoke-filled hovels usually made of wattle and clay. Rushes covered the floor. Pigs and poultry often shared the dwelling. Furniture was of the crudest quality. Food was simple. In prosperous times dried peas and wheaten bread were usual. Occasionally there was smoked bacon, fish or game; but fresh food was rare and milk, butter and cheese scarce. Spring was a lean time and fasting in Lent usually a necessity. There was a shortage of greenstuffs; general resistance to epidemics was low. Such relatively good living could not be taken for granted and the line that divided tolerable survival from abject poverty was a thin one. In times of scarcity even rural and urban craftsmen could be reduced to living on beans, peas, lentils and acorns: the labouring poor might come very close to starvation.

There was a close bond between town and countryside. Most of the county's towns, including Cambridge and Ely, were basically market centres for agricultural produce and despite piecemeal expansion had a rural air about them. They were small, smelly, unpaved and insanitary.

3

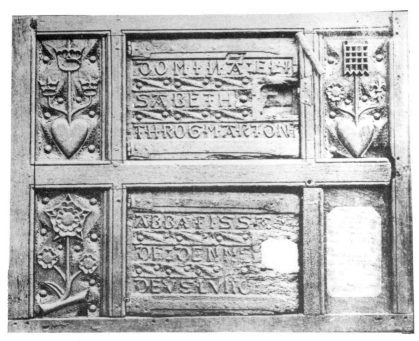

Old dole gate, Denny Abbey, Waterbeach.

Their houses, tenements and cottages were dirty and overcrowded and even in the sixteenth century it was common for Cambridge inhabitants to 'lay their muck, mire, dung, filth and other annoyances in the high streets'.[1] The problem of poverty was more obvious in urban areas; towns like Cambridge, Wisbech and Royston (which was partly in Hertfordshire) were havens for peasants who had fled from manor and lord, discharged soldiers, beggars, rogues and thieves. As many as one-third of the population of these towns might be below the status of wage-earner. The inevitable result was that poverty and begging was widespread and government interfered very little with it.

The Church played a prominent part in organizing poor-relief. Fêtes and sports, church ales and collections were commonplace in most parishes in the county. [2] The parish of Great St. Mary's in Cambridge built almshouses out of charitable bequests and regularly distributed benefactions to the poor. Cambridgeshire had twenty-eight monasteries and they also made a significant contribution. Though not as rich as the great Cistercian and Benedictine houses of the North of England, the Abbeys at Barnwell, Waterbeach, Anglesey, Ely, Thorney, Chatteris,

4

Spinney and Denny offered charity to all who required it. The four great orders of Friars also had houses in Cambridge. [3]

Not many folk, of course, were within daily reach of[1] such assistance. Probably of more importance to the poor of the county, most of whom lived in small, isolated rural parishes, were the gilds. Almost every village possessed one. The almshouse or gildhall, as at Whittlesford and Meldreth, became the village poorhouse of a later age. Ely had eleven socio-religious gilds in 1389, Cambridge had eight, and Bottisham seven. Many of these gilds were extremely well-endowed, often possessing hundreds of acres of land. [4] In Wisbech the town government evolved from its most famous gild—the Gild of the Holy Trinity—and it has been argued that the early history of the town is basically the history of its gild. It managed charitable bequests, provided a school, and in 1477 built an almshouse. Gild members who fell into poverty were assisted by the fraternity—as were widows and orphans. [5]

In an imaginary society where everybody lived in manor, village or town such a system might have proved sufficient. But medieval society was not static. In Cambridgeshire and elsewhere there were always mobile groups to be considered—the landless and homeless, beggars and vagrants, harlots and thieves, gypsies and outlaws. [6] The authorities inevitably saw these as a threat to law and order and endeavoured to supervise and control their movements. Vagrants often posed as University undergraduates and, as a result, a new element was added to

Swaffham Bulbeck Benedictine Nunnery.

the struggle between Town and Gown as each strove for control over powers of search and punishment. The town itself was particularly vulnerable to the influx of wandering beggars. Situated on the edge of the Fens, it also lay on the Great North Road out of London. The numerous open villages and wide stretches of uninhabited fen encouraged outsiders: Sturbridge Fair also attracted hundreds of vagrants to the area every year. Vagrancy regulations in Cambridge and Wisbech were, therefore, often linked with ordinances concerning plague for, as carriers of virulent diseases, wandering beggars, 'scholars', and 'pilgrims' were especially suspect. [7] Consequently, even before the Tudor period, these groups became identified as undesirables and were treated by town and county magistrates as the petty criminals they almost invariably were. [8]

❧ 2 ❧
Tudor Poor Relief

With the passing of the Middle Ages, the number of destitute in urban and rural areas increased. In many ways the Black Death of 1348-49 was the turning-point. It dealt a severe blow to serfdom and with the subsequent decline in population many landowners, desperate for labour, turned from arable to pasture farming. Despite the Statute of Labourers of 1351, designed to force every able-bodied man to work at pre-plague wage levels, peasants fled from the manors and sought more profitable work elsewhere. Many clearly preferred the insecurity of the roads to the servitude of villeinage. In the fifteenth century their numbers were swelled by a more dangerous group—ex-soldiers from the Hundred Years' War—and these were later joined by the baronial retainers disbanded after the Wars of the Roses. The old sources of charity were incapable of dealing with these increasing numbers. Meanwhile, the gilds were in decay and the monasteries were soon to disappear in the turmoil of Henry VIII's Reformation. [9] The Tudor monarchs, unsure of their throne, quickly decided that in the interests of peace and security they would have to tackle the problem of poverty. [10]

But who were the poor? This was not easily answered, for there were many kinds of poverty and each demanded different responses. The most obvious group were the aged and sick, the orphaned and disabled, the blind and the insane. Nobody denied that they needed help, but

Men in stocks.

what of those unemployed through no fault of their own? And what about the wandering vagrants, rogues and vagabonds? Clearly, poverty involved not only the poor but also the sick and often the unemployed. At first the Tudor government saw only two sides of the problem—the deserving and undeserving poor. They decided that the deserving or 'impotent' poor were to be given licences to beg. This was the Tudor equivalent to a pension and so a form of elementary classification had to be devised. By 1536 Cambridge corporation was registering and making badges 'for the pore folks to wer'. [11] Able-bodied beggars and vagrants, however, were believed to be lazy, preferring idleness to employment. Punishment appearing to be the only answer to such wilful conduct, a law of 1531 enacted that every vagrant caught begging without a licence should be 'tied to the end of a cart naked and beaten with whips throughout the same market town or place till his body be bloody'. [12] Undergraduates found begging were to be whipped and imprisoned in the stocks. This early legislation proved ineffective and precipitated a particularly savage Act in the stormy years of the reign of Edward VI. This stipulated that every sturdy vagrant discovered begging should be branded with the letter V for vagabond and compelled to work as a slave for his captors for two years. Although the Act was quickly repealed, throughout the century, thousands were whipped and hundreds burned through the ear.

The basic weakness of these early attempts to deal with poverty was the lack of local funds, of information about the numbers of poor, and of skilled administrators. The collection of sufficient funds also proved to be a major and persistent problem. By mid-century the more progressive towns evolved a system of voluntary levies based on property. [13] In Cambridge (and Wisbech) the first levy was occasioned by the coincidence of a plague and a bad harvest in 1556. Town and University authorities combined to organise compulsory collections in each of the town's parishes, where lists of the deserving poor were drawn up. Begging without a licence was prohibited and to prevent indiscriminate alms-giving certain townsmen were appointed as 'watchers for strange beggeres'. [14] Parliament followed the lead of the localities. At first it had seen only the dangers inherent in social instability and unrest and therefore had reacted repressively but it soon acknowledged the benefits of rating and classification.

In 1572, Elizabeth's government, impressed by these urban initiatives, ordered a compulsory national levy and in this way the national poor-rate was established. Justices of the Peace were now given the task of assessing parishes, appointing overseers of the poor, and supervising the distribution of relief.[15] No provision was made for vagrants. These 'undeserving poor' were still to be whipped and branded; after repeated offences they could even be hanged. However, an Act of 1576 introduced the new concept of setting the unemployed to work in Houses of Correction, where stocks of hemp, flax and wool were ordered to be set aside for their use. These houses, which despite their titles were basically charitable institutions, were the forerunners of later workhouses. Cambridge did not respond to this legislation until 1596. The main preoccupation of the town was in finding more efficient methods of collecting the poor-rate, supervising food supplies in years of bad harvests and building a hospital for the destitute.

Wisbech adopted a much more humane policy towards the poor of the town. During this period its progressive town corporation adopted a mixture of voluntary and semi-voluntary methods to relieve those in distress through no fault of their own. This generosity applied even to vagrants. They were given help and then simply moved on. Whereas Cambridge had continually to be spurred by exhortations from the Privy Council in London, Wisbech was spared such unwelcome attention. As at Cambridge, it was the occurrence of plague and dearth which prompted the levying of the first compulsory town poor-rate in 1585, but the emphasis appeared to remain on the more traditional type of voluntary contributions. In this respect Wisbech was unique in the county and this policy, coupled with the efficient administration of the 'Ten Men' (the capital burgesses) made it a model municipality in matters of poor-relief. [16]

Linton organised its system of poor-relief along similar lines. By the late 1570s, collectors were rendering an annual account of monies collected to the parish vestry. To these were added donations, bequests and endowments. An institution called the 'Taske House' was founded and served as a kind of workhouse for the poor of the surrounding area. Within a few years it degenerated into little more than a poorhouse for the impotent poor of the village, who were also given temporary accommodation in part of the old gildhall. Many of the larger rural villages in the county (such as Sawston and Littleport) dealt with the poor similarly. On the whole they tended to mix medieval and Tudor forms of relief and generally tried to mitigate the more repressive elements in the Tudor system. [17]

Though Cambridgeshire was not at the centre of sixteenth century social change it is important to remember the factors that stimulated Tudor legislation on poverty. Much rural distress was occasioned by the enclosure of land for pasture. Sir Thomas More, in his *Utopia*, commenting on the consequent social disruption and unemployment, observed: 'Your sheep that were wont to be so meek and tame, and so small eaters, now, as I hear say, be become so great devourers and so wild, that they eat up, and swallow down the very men themselves'. The effects of a rising population, a five-fold price inflation, plague, the upheaval of the Henrician Reformation and the Elizabethan wars against Spain all aggravated Tudor fears of social instability. Rebellions such as Robert Ket's in Norfolk and its Cambridge counterpart in 1549 were dangerous and expensive to suppress. [18] Possessing neither a police force nor a standing army, the government was compelled to intervene to maintain law and order. Doubtless the numbers of vagrants were exaggerated, but even if they numbered only 20,000 in a population of approximately three million, they could constitute a major headache for Tudor government and society. Though the Church continued to encourage corporate and individual acts of charity, and Protestant businessmen fostered social works and charitable foundations as readily as their Catholic forbears, it soon became clear that this mixture of religious and private charity was incapable of solving what appeared to be an ever-growing problem. [19]

Vagrant whipped through the streets, from R. Holinshed's *Chronicles*, 1577.

In the unhappy closing decade of the century, when it was alleged that the poor were actually dying of starvation in parts of the Midlands, an apprehensive Tudor government fashioned the existing systems of poor-relief into a code. Some of the best brains of the day inspired it: William Burghley, Queen Elizabeth's chief minister, Archbishop Whitgift, Sir Francis Bacon and Sir Robert Wroth. They considered a long list of Commons' proposals and drew up a bill in 1597-98 which both Houses of Parliament approved. It was designed as an experiment but was re-enacted in all its essentials in 1601 (the famous 43rd of Elizabeth) and became the basis of the Poor Law until the Amendment Act of 1834.

In fact there was little that was entirely new in the 1601 Act:[20] it was merely a codification of laws already in existence. It stipulated that each parish was to be responsible for its own poor; administration was to be in the hands of the churchwardens and overseers; and the poor-rate was to be national. The aged, sick, disabled and blind were to be maintained and housed out of parish funds. Work was to be provided for the willing able-bodied and a stock of wool, flax and hemp, kept by parish overseers for the purpose. Sturdy beggars were to be arrested and compelled to work in the Houses of Correction or simply thrown into gaol. Pauper children were to be apprenticed so that they might grow up as self-supporting citizens. Wandering abroad and begging, with or without a licence, was to be punished as roguery. Those convicted were to be whipped and sent back to the parishes in which they were born. As early as 1588 there is recorded in Cambridge a sum spent 'for ye carrynge of a blind woman out of towne, by the commandement of Mister Maior'. [21] Churchwardens and overseers were to meet at least monthly and parish poor accounts were to be submitted for audit annually to two Justices, who supervised the workings of the whole system.

Voluntary contributions were not discouraged and indeed continued to augment existing arrangements, but this measure of state interference and control ushered in a new era in the history of English poor-relief. However, we must not give too much credit to Tudor statesmen for the creation of this system, since many local corporations, among them Cambridge, Wisbech and Norwich, had acted well in advance of, and had anticipated most of the provisions of, the Elizabethan Poor Law. The passage of two centuries produced social and economic changes that eventually rendered the Act obsolete but in 1601 England could boast of a more enlightened and efficient system of poor-relief than any other country in Europe. [22]

❧ 3 ❧
Poor Relief under the Stuarts

The national system evolved in 1601 may have been more impressive on paper than in performance because the first fifty years of the seventeenth century were depressing years for the labouring poor in East Anglia. Their life-style and circumstances probably deteriorated during this period. With the cloth industry in decline, the resultant unemployment, combined with Puritanism, spread throughout the region disaffection exacerbated by the Civil War as the county notables struggled against political uncertainty, plague, bad harvests and economic slump. [23] Prior to the Civil War, town and county authorities, harassed as never before by the Privy Council, were endeavouring to introduce the 1601 Act. [24] Disappointingly, compulsory poor-rates were not a complete solution to the ever-growing problem of poverty.

In Cambridge the poorer parishes, such as St. Giles, St. Andrew and Holy Trinity, often failed to raise the sums assessed. Extra rates were occasionally levied to make up the deficit. Parishes were also beginning to dispute the settlement bounds and the question of who were, or were not, entitled to relief. For example, only part of the Falcon Inn lay in the parish of Great St. Mary's. [25] Accordingly vestry officials of adjacent parishes carefully housed any unfortunate poor on that side of the Inn so that the claim for relief (usually disputed) was on Great St. Mary's. Unemployed newcomers from the rural areas were also vigorously hunted and removed under Privy Council directives against plague, but primarily in an effort to keep down the rates.

There was much discussion also about the desirability of a House of Correction. In 1628 Thomas Hobson, the famous carrier, offered land in the Parish of St. Andrew's outside Barnwell Gate for the building of one. However, it took the outbreak of a virulent plague in 1630, to stimulate the appointed trustees into action. Almost 3000 people claimed relief as local farmers refused to bring their produce to market. London and Norwich helped generously. With the extra funds thus made available, plus an additional sum bequeathed by Hobson, the House of Correction was built. A salary of £30 per annum was made available for the keeper to look after the idle and impotent poor of the town. A stock of wool and flax was also provided to set them to work. [26] This dual nature of the workhouse (both punitive and reformatory) was characteristic more of the urban than of the rural scene. Most of the county Houses were ill-equipped and supervised: in reality they were little better than detention centres. The recalcitrant, criminal poor of the county were sent to the central House of Correction at Chesterton.

The Civil War, with Justices of the Peace often fighting on opposing sides, hampered the administration of the Poor Law; Privy Council supervision almost ceased. From 1642 Cambridge was the headquarters of the Eastern Association and consequently suffered very directly from the presence of troops. There was continual sickness and poverty and inability to collect rates from the poorer parishes. [27] Privation was aggravated by official negligence. A legacy of £200 left by a benefactor in 1642 for Hobson's workhouse was unused for four years while Town and Gown wrangled over right of precedence in the deed.

Fortunately, private charity did not dry up; in fact there was more in the first forty years of the seventeenth century than in the whole of the preceding century. [28] Hobson's endowment of a workhouse was not the only major benefaction in Cambridge. The University trebled its annual voluntary contribution for the maintenance of the poor. In 1614 Stephen Perse left houses for six poor women in addition to founding a free school. William Baldwin left £100 for apprenticing poor children and Henry Wray a bequest to build an almshouse for eight poor widows in 1628. Outside the scope of the national system, churchwardens also continued to give supplementary aid. In 1619 thirty-one individuals in the town were helped. An old man 'for a losse by fire' received

Knight and Mortlock's almhouses, Cambridge 1647; rebuilt 1818.

18d., and 8s. was spent on 'coles to the poore'. The sum of 2s. was paid for 'the burial of John Harrison, a poore man'. Churchwardens at Ely, who possessed a status higher than that of overseers, were conscientious and vigilant. They apprenticed children, provided employment for the able-bodied, and initiated projects for the unemployed. [29]

Wisbech Corporation, in the absence of Privy Council interference, continued to play a bigger part in the administration of poor relief than did the town parishes, and compulsory relief merely supplemented other sources of income. These progressive town fathers concentrated on the task of providing work for the unemployed; by the use of subsidies they encouraged local employers to hire the willing, able-bodied poor. Consequently even more unemployed were attracted to the town from the surrounding areas. In 1614, part of the House of Correction was set aside for the training of poor children. On the other hand, the town Bridewell was used as a gaol for the wandering vagabonds of the whole northern part of the county. Prior to the Civil War, even the new Town Hall was used as a workhouse in an effort to bring the problem under control. The municipal activity of its burgesses contrasted sharply with the inefficiency of its churchwardens and parish overseers who appeared content to do very little. Four almshouses were bequeathed to the Corporation in 1616, and £300 was left by Dr. Watson for a similar purpose in 1631. The 'Ten Men' allowed 20s. to a poor widow in 1648 because 'she had not been relieved by the overseers' and granted 5s. to one Charity Russell 'for curing Pierson's head, 2s.6d. more when safe and whole'—an unusual and interesting form of payment by results. [30]

At Linton the old task house and gildhall continued to be used as a workhouse and lodging-house for the poor but stocks of flax and hemp were also given to homeworkers. [31] The same system existed at Whittlesford but here the inmates of the gildhall were almost all old folk and widows, most of whom were employed in spinning. In some other parishes, such as Littleport, there is no evidence of any communal building for the poor, and home-spinning tended to be the norm. Other parishes, such as Sawston and Ickleton, managed to succour their poor on benefactions only. Throughout the county, methods of poor-rate collection, patterns of expenditure and distribution of endowments varied enormously. [32]

Inevitably in the years after the Civil War, vagrancy of every description (of demobilised soldiers, jobbing migrants, harlots, thieves) grew alarmingly. Gregory King estimated that a quarter of the total population of 5.5 million was in a state of poverty and that in times of distress this figure could grow to half. The better-regulated parishes, meaning those which most conscientiously carried out their obligation to the poor, proved an ever-increasing attraction to those in need and the result was the Act of Settlement of 1662. [33] This Act authorised every parish to move on, within forty days, any immigrant who appeared likely to become a burden to it. According to the legislators, overseers had neglected their duty of providing work; one at Coton, for example, was sued for retaining money that should have been used to employ the poor. For a similar offence three overseers at Cottenham were each fined 33s.4d. They brazenly paid the fine out of the poor rates. [34]

The Act itself was expensive to operate and was undoubtedly the cause of much misery and brutality as every parish sought to avoid liabilities that could be transferred elsewhere. A group of hardened vagabonds, male and female, taken at Linton in 1663 were branded on the shoulder with the letter R for rogue before being returned to their place of settlement. [35] At St. Clement's in Cambridge the churchwardens gave 'a Marriage Present and Fees to Widow Arnold, by which we got rid of her in the family way'. [36] An unexpected effect was to discourage married men from leaving their parishes in an effort to find work. A new kind of serfdom was thus imposed on the poor. They were compelled to remain in their village or town, not because they were forbidden to leave, but because no other parish would accept responsibility for them. In an effort to overcome this, certificates were often

14

issued to migrant workmen by the parish accepting liability in the matter of settlement. The illegal practice of distributing 'walking passes' also developed; by the late eighteenth century a permit to travel throughout the county was comparatively easy to acquire. [37]

The really important part of the Act of 1662 was the granting of arbitrary power to remove the poor on the verdict of two Justices of the Peace. This promoted injustice and oppression, not to mention expense. Overseers vigorously contested settlement and the J.P.s usually allied themselves with parochial authority. Removals and counter-removals of the unhappy victims of the Act abounded and were occasionally outrageous. In Cambridgeshire between 1704 and 1708 the Loader family, a widowed mother and her three children, were removed and counter-removed no fewer than seven times. The unfortunate mother died before a final decision on settlement was reached and her orphaned children were promptly put into pauper apprenticeship. [38] Removal of a pauper usually awaited negotiation between contending parishes but some over-zealous officials were often unwilling to wait. On one occasion, in St. Edward's Parish, Cambridge, such undue haste had tragic results.

In that parish the respectable and hard-working Widow Samwell managed to maintain herself and her two children, until one was stricken with smallpox, and the mother was forced to give up her employment. The unsympathetic overseer quickly arraigned her before the Justices and argued that her place of settlement was at Battle in Sussex. A waggon was hired; in the middle of winter the unfortunate family was put on the road. By the time the waggon reached the outskirts of North London one of the children had died. At Battle overseers buried the dead child and provided food and shelter for the family. It was soon discovered that Battle was not the widow's parish and, as expenses for wrongful removal were recoverable, the Battle authorities inoculated the child and provided clothes and groceries, confident of recovering all the expenses incurred. The overseers at St. Edward's suddenly realised their mistake and promptly arranged for the widow to be returned. The total expenditure in transport, burial, maintenance and lawyers' fees would have maintained the whole family in Cambridge for two years! [39] In the years between 1660 and 1831 two thirds of the time of the County Bench was taken up with 945 appeals against removal orders which came before them, a third of which related to married men with families. Certain classes of people were most often concerned: married men, widows and pregnant single women. [40] The account books of parish overseers are filled with examples of these unfortunate

A curious group of buildings in Cambridge. (Pleasure is represented by the Fountain Public House; Law and order by the Police Station; Morality by Hobson's Spinning House and Religion by St. Andrew's Street Chapel).

people, many of whom were transported abroad to England's labour-hungry plantations in America.

Similarly, since the place of settlement of a bastard was the place of birth, overseers showed little mercy and great industry in moving pregnant single women outside the confines of the parish. In order to secure the parish against absconding fathers, the Act allowed distraint of goods, for it was considered that most fathers escaped too easily. As the number of bastardy suits rose, the magistrates adopted the policy of pursuing only those who appeared likely to pay, such as farmers, millers, publicans and undergraduates. Many complaints of non-payment were also made against unscrupulous overseers and the parish of Bourn, for example, which received £29 from unmarried fathers in 1830, paid out only £22 in aid. Bastardy payments, it appears, were a great source of temptation to many a parish overseer. Fathers who absconded and were apprehended and returned to the parish, according to the poet Crabbe, often found the vicar waiting, offering the wronged woman with one hand and a warrant for arrest with the other:

> Next at our altar stand a luckless pair
> Brought by strong passions and a warrant there.

The choice was either church or gaol and forced marriages, especially between very youthful parties, became common in the decades before 1834. [41]

There is no doubt that overseers saw large families as a threat to the

16

rates and married men were rarely given settlement or work in other parishes. As a result, men made strenuous efforts to avoid marriage and this led to an alleged increase in immorality. During the Napoleonic Wars and the depressed years that followed, bastardy cases in the county increased dramatically from 37 cases between 1757 and 1771 to 365 for the years between 1796 and 1830. [42] Most parishes were at a loss for a remedy but the overseers for Histon and Fowlmere suggested that if maintenance were to fall entirely on the mother, they would be less generous with their favours and fewer bastards would be born. [43]

❦ 4 ❦
The Workhouses of Cambridgeshire

In the opinion of the legislators of 1662, it was failure to provide employment that encouraged mobility among the destitute. Urban employment was becoming a serious problem, and from the discussion it provoked in the late seventeenth century emerged the concept of the profitable employment of the poor. Nevertheless, in spite of the consternation caused by the Plague of 1665-66 there was no expansion of the activity of Hobson's workhouse (or the Spinning House as it was now called). Some towns such as Wisbech concentrating on schemes to help the young unemployed founded Industrial or Charity Schools and encouraged local employers to hire out the able-bodied unemployed at subsidised rates. [44]

By the beginning of the eighteenth century the concept of profitable employment appeared to have failed. The able-bodied generally left the workhouses as quickly as possible; soon these housed only the sick, widows, orphans and the totally destitute, as at Cottenham, Meldreth and Linton where the poorhouse rather than the workhouse was characteristic. However, in Cambridge and elsewhere the poorhouses were rarely institutions. Often they were merely cottages or large buildings in which no provision was made for work, diet, health or discipline. Poorhouse and workhouse were sometimes combined as they were in the gildhall at Whittlesford and Hobson's workhouse in Cambridge. [45] There were similar institutions at Dullingham and Swavesey. Where there were none, the poor were boarded out at ratepayers' expense.

In 1722, after some initial experiments at Bristol and Norwich (and locally at Wisbech), the Government passed the Workhouse Act. Parochial authorities were empowered to buy land for the building of workhouses in the hope that they would provide training and work as well as accommodation. They could also apply what became known in the nineteenth century as the workhouse test: anybody that refused to enter the house would be denied public assistance. The Act also recognised the desirability of joint action by the smaller parishes. Wisbech had begun to build its workhouse in 1720. It was completed in 1722 at a cost of £2000 and soon had eighty, apparently industrious and well-fed, inmates. Brewing, baking and spinning were carried out on the premises. Old and young of the same sex slept two or three to a bed in segregated rooms. Their diet was good, including beef, dumplings, porridge, bread and cheese. The Master and Mistress were paid a fixed salary to try to ensure efficient administration of the house. Chatteris and Ely, impressed by the apparent success of their fen neighbour's scheme, soon began to prepare one of their own. Ely's was operational in 1729 and, with the full support of the townspeople, pursued a generous policy, even to the extent of supplying the inmates with a ration of tobacco during the troubled years of the Napoleonic War.

Administration was complicated in Cambridge because of the division of the town into fourteen unequal parishes with populations ranging from 200 to 700 inhabitants. In addition to the Spinning House, most of these parishes already had a mixture of almshouses or poorhouses. A corporation proposal for the building of a workhouse in 1727 was not taken up primarily because many townsmen distrusted the corporation and the richer parishes were reluctant to subsidise those that were poorer and more populous. The result was that most parishes decided to build or acquire their own workhouses. In 1734 Great St. Mary's appointed a committee to inquire into the possibility of buying a house to serve as a workhouse in Sparrow Lane. The committee, however, recommended the purchase of some cottages in Slaughterhouse Lane, which were later acquired. St. Bene't's, on the other hand, rented for £10 per annum a building which they used as a workhouse from 1747. St. Andrew the Great also adopted a similar policy in 1756. [47]

The main characteristics of these little parochial workhouses, as described in their inventories, were fairly common. There was usually an officer's room, a kitchen, bathroom and workroom and a few communal bedrooms. Furniture, crockery and cooking utensils were simple. Pails and wash-troughs were provided for ablutions. Spinning-wheels were usually installed in the workroom. Diet appears to have been

St. Andrew the Great Workhouse,
St. Tibb's Row, Cambridge.

reasonable in quality and fairly plentiful. The weekly workhouse account for the eight or nine inmates of St. Botolph's in 1746 included a small amount of butter, oatmeal, bread, 12 lbs. of cheese, 30 lbs. of beef, and some vegetables. The total cost of the provisions, plus two bushels of coal, amounted to £1 2s. Outdoor relief continued to be given and soon it was only the aged, orphaned and sick that inhabited workhouses. Work also disappeared from most of their programmes and by the end of the eighteenth century many houses were open only inter- mittently. [48]

These stark details obviously hid the harsher realities of workhouse existence and, although the workhouse may have been a refuge from life's worst calamities, the destitute were reluctant to enter them. Other items of expenditure seemingly confirm the worst fears of the poor, for example, St. Clement's paid £1 1s. for rat poison in 1811, a suggestively large amount. [49] Letters to the *Cambridge Chronicle* in the 1750s are critical of general workhouse provision and there was further discussion between Town, Gown and the parishes about the possibility of providing a general town workhouse. One vigorous supporter of the plan was the Rev. John Micklebourgh, Vicar of St. Andrew's. In 1751 he delivered a famous (and very informative) sermon on the need for a general work- house. The Mayor and Corporation were present, and had to listen to a trenchant attack on 'profligate lazy vagrants...whose misery is deserved' and also on the parish workhouses which Micklebourgh claimed were 'nurseries of laziness, nastiness and vice...Houses of Play and Debauchery and not Houses of Work'. [50] The University urged the Corporation to consider a new scheme but, on such a thorny subject, what scheme could be acceptable to the parishes or to the town generally?

The parliamentary returns on a workhouse enquiry in 1776 inform us that the total number of inmates in parish workhouses in that year was 140. [51] Many of these, such as Goody Bridges, the troublesome, mentally-deranged widow, were famous Cambridge eccentrics. In later years one of the best known was Jemmy Gordon, once a successful attorney before he destroyed his career by extravagant spending on clothes and drink. Dressed in a general's cast-off uniform, topped with an admiral's hat, he roamed the streets of Cambridge, singing and reciting verse. Now, mentally unsound but tolerantly indulged by the inhabitants of the town, he spent the remainder of his life in and out of the workhouse until in a drunken state, he slipped off the ladder of an outhouse at the rear of the Hoop Inn. After weeks of suffering he died in one of the parish workhouses. [52]

Linton built a workhouse in 1737 but, unlike those in Cambridge, it organised a considerable amount of spinning for which there was a ready market in the area. The seventeen inmates were contracted to the Master at 1s.9d. per head, a sum which at eighteenth century prices could barely have prevented starvation. Royston had a far less efficiently managed workhouse, primarily because its geographical location rendered it particularly susceptible to sudden influxes, and equally sudden departures, of vagrants. In 1774 there were twenty-six paupers in the house. These were soon joined by fourteen others (mostly children) who were promptly abandoned by their parents. Little work was done in the children's workroom but some of the older children were contracted to work on a nearby farm (the property of the overseer) at the exploitive rate of 4d. per week, the normal rate for agricultural labourers at the time being at least 6d. per day. [53]

Sawston and Bottisham never possessed a workhouse. Sawston had a poorhouse accommodating in 1791 eight widows, three old men and one orphan. They supported themselves on a personal parish allowance of 2s. per week. Littleport did not consider a workhouse necessary until 1768, but Soham had the largest workhouse in the county. It had sixty residents in 1776; over a quarter of its income came from spinning. James Chambers, a local poet, graphically describes the oppressiveness of workhouse life at the time:

> By day must I dwell where there's many a wheel,
> And female employed to sit down and reel,
> A post with two ringles is fixed in the wall,
> Where orphans, when lasted, loud for mercy do call,
> Deprived of fresh air, I must there commence spinner,
> If I fail of my task I lose a hot dinner;
> Perhaps at the whipping post then shall be flogged,
> And lest I escape my leg must be clogged.
> While tyrants oppress I must still be their slave,
> And cruelly used, tho' well I behave:
> Midst swearing and brawling my days I must spend,
> In sorrow and anguish my days I must end. [54]

While the proportion of parishes which had a workhouse was only one in ten in the county, it was one in three in the Isle of Ely. In 1776 there were only 331 inmates in county workhouses, whereas there were almost double that number in the Isle. Wisbech housed 150, March 100, Whittlesey 90, Ely 80, and Thorney 60. Conditions in the workhouses were less oppressive in the Isle; little work was produced. The reasons for this were more likely administrative than human. Few people wanted the task of supervising the able-bodied, aged, orphaned and insane or organising them for work. By the late eighteenth-century Hobson's workhouse in Cambridge had become a Bridewell (or prison) possessing cells with iron gratings on the doors and windows. In 1815 it was alleged that in St. Andrew's workhouse the consumption of small beer 'exceeded all discretion'. In the parishes of St. Edward's and St. Giles' it was necessary to add special barred rooms to house the violent and insane. [55]

To what extent the Poor Laws of the eighteenth century in town and county relieved unemployment, underpay or destitution is almost impossible to calculate. But the range of relief was demonstrably widened during the century. Pauper children were boarded out, supplementary relief was given to alleviate the burden of high rents and the high cost of food, winter fuel and clothes. Care of the sick was also extended and doctors employed by the parish on contract. It is clear that conditions varied enormously and the law was often either indifferently or harshly administered. However, this was a hard age, in which women were still whipped, criminals lodged in hulks and sailors flogged to death. Violence was taken for granted. Boys whether of Eton or the workhouse were treated brutally. Hanging, bear-baiting and cock-fighting were still popular spectacles. The poor had their compensations—such as communal fellowship, hard drinking and, paradoxically enough, chapel-going, but the attitude to the poor which carried most weight was inevitably harsh. There was much talk about the laziness of the poor. It was suggested that dear food was not a bad thing; it could be a deterrent to idleness and excessive gin-drinking, evils immortalised by Hogarth's *Gin Lane*. Nevertheless, for all its deficiencies, the Poor Law remained the best, almost the only, institution of its kind in Europe. [56]

❧ 5 ❧
The Road to 1834

After centuries of slow growth, England, from the middle of the eighteenth century, experienced rapid agrarian and industrial changes which, to both contemporaries and recent historians, appeared revolutionary. In agriculture the external sign of change was the disappearance of the old, open, hedgeless fields now being enclosed into the neatly-patterned squares still familiar today. Enclosure of this type (and drainage schemes in the Fens) had been going on for centuries. But under the stimulus of a sharply rising population (which grew from an estimated 5 million in 1700 to almost 18 million by 1851) and of the extra demand for food occasioned by the Napoleonic War, the whole process quickened. [57]

This agrarian revolution may have been economically desirable; too often it was socially disastrous. The poor suffered most. They were driven off the land; occasionally their cottages were pulled down. They lost their rights of common. And although some may have benefitted from the increasing possibilities of employment, such as hedging and ditching, this gain was often ephemeral. What was new for the poor of the countryside was their utter dependence on employment for their daily bread. Under the old system the right of gleaning after harvest, the use of common and waste for poultry, firewood and game, occasional spinning at home, could mean the difference between managing and starving. These buffers against poverty had now gone. It was this change in status, this loss of self-reliance, that caused much of the demoralisation so widespread in the decades before 1834. [58] Previously, recourse to the Poor Law was occasional and only in times of severe distress: now it was increasingly becoming the alternative to work. These changes produced a crisis in the administration of poor-relief as national expenditure on poverty grew from £1.5 million in 1776 to

£7 million by 1831 —just over 10s. per head of the poor population. [59]

The most significant development in the years after 1780 in Cambridgeshire was the growth of outdoor relief. Gilbert's Act of 1782 encouraged the grouping of parishes into Unions for the better administration of poor-relief but no Gilbert Unions were ever formed in the county. Cambridge retained its parochial workhouses, but by now most of those still open were little better than badly-run lodging houses. Any notion of the profitable employment of inmates had long since been abandoned: the total workhouse population of the town in 1804 was only 108. Meanwhile the numbers receiving outdoor relief were almost 500. By 1834 the workhouse population had risen to 150; those being relieved outside the workhouse reached ten times that number. [60]

Of course, outdoor relief was not a new development in Cambridgeshire. The deserving poor had always been selected by the overseers for relief, and the undeserving ruthlessly weeded out, but in almost every parish the rise in expenditure was marked. In Haslingfield, for example, expenditure rose from £85 in 1776 to £775 in 1814. There was also relief in kind and cash for coal and clothing in winter. [61] In Bottisham the overseers distributed doles of wheat, barley and rye. Though workhouse employment appeared to have ceased, the parishes of Linton,

PARISH OF THE HOLY TRINITY.

Orders and Regulations

TO BE OBSERVED BY

All Paupers who are admitted into the Parish House.

1. That the Governor examine all Paupers previous to their admission into this House.

2. That no Pauper be allowed to go out of the House without leave from the Governor.

3. That every Pauper shall be down stairs by six o'clock in the morning (unless prevented by illness), and in bed by nine o'clock in the evening, from Lady-Day till Michaelmas; and from Michaelmas to Lady-Day every one shall be down by seven o'clock in the morning, and in bed by eight o'clock in the evening.

4. That no smoking be allowed at any time.

5. That those Paupers who are able shall go out to work, of which they must give an account to the Governor. The Men shall be allowed to retain one-fourth, and the Women one-half of their earnings; the remainder to be given to the Governess, who shall keep an account of the same in a book.

6. That every Pauper shall attend Divine Service twice on the Sabbath Day; and those who refuse to comply with this order shall not be allowed any dinner on that day.

7. That if any Pauper shall use profane, obscene, or abusive language, insult the Governor or Governess, or refuse to obey any of the above or following Regulations, he or she shall be reported to the Parish Officers to be dealt with accordingly.

8. That in case any Pauper, who is an inmate of this House, get intoxicated, he or she shall be reported to the Parish Officers on the following morning by the Governor, in order to be punished as the law directs.

9. That the Governor shall read grace every day before and after dinner.

10. That the Governor shall also read morning and evening prayers every day.

PRINTED BY WESTON HATFIELD, SIDNEY-STREET.

Holy Trinity Workhouse, Cambridge, orders and regulations.

Fowlmere and Soham still tried to provide work for the poor in the declining textile trade. At Histon in 1799 a quantity of raw wool was stored in the workhouse for distribution to poor outworkers. Other parishes did occasionally provide work, such as breaking and sifting gravel, carting stones and making road repairs. In 1834 two-thirds of the money earned by labourers on the road, was paid as relief by the parish. [62] Fair wages paid to independent labourers properly supervised seemed to have ceased. The policy of supplementing wages out of rates had already begun.

The 1790s were difficult years for the poor in Cambridgeshire. The war with France was going badly, harvests were rarely good and unemployment and inflation led to rumours of revolution among agricultural labourers. The University and corporation voted funds for the prosecution of forestallers and monopolisers. Village soup kitchens were set up in times of acute distress. This kind of philanthropic exercise was often very generous. In December 1800 almost £1200 was subscribed in Cambridge for soup for the poor. The activity obviously satisfied Christian consciences. More importantly, it guaranteed some form of social control. Nevertheless, food riots were common, and bread and flour were often seized. On one occasion in 1795 they were reclaimed only when the magistrates agreed to sell, the loaves made from the confiscated flour at 6d. each. [63] It was generally felt that not enough was being done to alleviate hardship: letters to the local newspaper complained that the poor of the town were in 'inconceivable distress'. [64]

In such exceptional circumstances new methods had to be considered, for not only were the unemployed to be sustained, but those in work were also in desperate need because of food shortages and high prices. The county notables of the eighteenth century could hardly be described as caring philanthropists, but they would all agree that the independent labourer was entitled to a minimum wage and, those unable to find work, to a minimum level of subsistence. In the light of such vaguely-felt views the magistrates at Berkshire, meeting at the Pelican Inn at Speenhamland in 1795, attempted to change the Poor Law from an institution not so much to succour the poor as to ensure a living wage for agricultural labourers. A minimum wage, linked to the prevailing price of bread, was fixed; if labourers' earnings fell below that amount it was to be supplemented from the poor rates. Additional payments were made for wives and children. Each district adopted its own scale: not all gave relief in money. [65] As we have already seen, this was not a new idea in Cambridgeshire but it took some time to be generally adopted.

24

Chatteris Jan.y 6.th 1790

At a vestry held this day at the Parish Church
in Chatteris aforesaid by Appointment

Present {
Tho.s Payne   W.m Osborn   John Byfield
Tho.s Quinsee   Tho.s Peet   Tho.s Kidd
}

Ordered that this Meeting do Immediately adjourn
to be holden at the Cross Keys Inn in Chatteris afs.d

Tho.s Payne   W.m Osborn   John Byfield
Tho.s Quinsee   Tho.s his mark Peet   Tho.s Shedd

Met according to adjournment and proceeded to business.
The Assessment of the Poor's Rate being perused
Ordered that it be and is ~~hereby~~ allowed and passed
by this vestry.

Ordered that the Overseers do get the new
work House & furniture, Insured for three Hundred
Pounds

Ordered that the W.d Read be allowed eighteen pence
a week.

Ordered that the Overseers do with Cart and Horse
take the wid.w Hill's Daughter to St Ives next monday
and take the advice and assistance of Doct.r ~~Fraser~~
Fraser respecting her present complaint.

Tho.s Flaunt   James Hunt   Robert Cave
W.m Osborn   John Byfield   Rob.t his R Ruston mark
Thomas Richardson   Tho.s his R Peet   W.m his mark Cawthorn
Tho.s Quinsee   Rich.d Ruston   Tho.s Payne
W.m Ruston
Tho.s Lemon

Overseers' accounts, Chatteris, 1790.

As early as 1783 the Justices at Whittlesford decided that every well-behaved, deserving family man should be allowed the price of five quartern loaves (each weighing 4 lbs. 4 oz.) a week, with two quartern loaves added for each member of his family. Married labourers in employment were to be guaranteed a minimum wage of 6s. a week. By the early 1790s the roundsman system was in operation in Sawston, Bottisham and Burwell and throughout the Isle of Ely. [66] Men were sent round the village with a ticket entitling them to employment at whatever rate the employer, usually a farmer, decided. The parish then made up the rate to 1s. a day. For those unable to find work, a few pence a day were deducted.

After Speenhamland the magistrates worked hard at devising a bread scale for the area but no common county scale was agreed until 1821. The Speenhamland scale fixed the minimum weekly income of a single man at approximately six quartern loaves a week, and allowed an additional three loaves for each member of his family if he were married. The Cambridgeshire scale was much less generous. Whereas Speenhamland allowed a married man with three children eighteen loaves a week, the Cambridge scale expected them to survive on eleven. A single man was allocated the equivalent price of 2½ lbs. of bread a day, yet a prisoner in the county gaol got 1½ lbs. a day plus his shelter. [67]

In spite of the teachings of Malthus, the meagre allowance offered to a married labourer would hardly encourage him to increase the size of his family in order to enjoy the extra benefits. The effects on the morale of the independent agricultural labourer was widely believed to be wholly detrimental. It pauperised, demoralised and immobilised him and ensured that he could hope to avoid starvation only in his own village and nowhere else in England.[68] It discriminated especially against the single man and small-family man and caused the poor-rates to soar without diminishing poverty. Though more and more stress in the 1820s was laid on poverty-stricken applicants being of good behaviour, the overseers and magistrates, fearful of riots and attacks on property were, according to John Denson of Waterbeach, more generous to the 'threatening' poor than to those who were genuinely in need but appeared less dangerous. Those who got relief were, in Denson's words, almost always 'servile, tale-bearing, dust-licking, canting and hypocritical'. [69]

Against such a background it is no surprise that riots occurred at Ely and Littleport in 1816. Desperate labourers smashed farm machinery, burnt barns and marched under a banner inscribed 'Bread or Blood'. The riots were ruthlessly suppressed and five of the leaders executed.

As the years went by more and more labourers were committed to the County Gaol under the Vagrancy Law for refusing to work at what they regarded as starvation wages.[70] County Magistrates and University authorities expressed concern 'at the extraordinary influx of Beggars and Vagrants, who constantly infest the streets, walks and Colleges'. A Society for the Suppression of Mendicity was founded in Cambridge in 1819.[71] There were riots at Sawston and Kirtling in 1822; declining conditions finally brought about the agricultural labourers' revolt of 1830.[72] Labourers' resentment was also directed against the large numbers of Scottish and Irish immigrants who, possessing vagrancy passes, appeared to be able to travel wherever they pleased without hindrance. Unrest was usually provoked by the arrival of Irish harvesters in the county. In 1821 an alleged increase in the numbers that farmers were employing caused a riot at Bassingbourn.[73] Many Irish were also reported at Cambridge, March, Thorney and Wisbech. Well over seventy per cent of the 500 vagrants who passed through Cambridge anually during the years before 1834 were said to be Irish. At harvest time they flocked to those parishes where there were ill-supervised workhouses and lodging-houses, such as the parishes of

Apprehension of Vagrants Notice, Stuntney near Ely, 1799.

Little St. Mary's and St. Clement's in Cambridge, and Whittlesford and March in the county. As many as ninety-five vagrants a week entered Cambridge during these harvesting weeks. [74]

Under such pressures the county administration of poor-relief had almost collapsed by 1830. Churchwardens neglected their responsibilities; monthly parish meetings were discontinued; overseers did everything possible to evade their unwelcome duties. The fine for refusing the office of overseer was raised from 10s. to 40s. The deserving poor were now given relief without question and the able-bodied given hand-outs without any suggestion of work being required. Alternatively they were herded together—unsupervised—in gravel-pits to labour or loiter as they thought fit. The paymaster for one area of Bottisham was himself a pauper. Continuing to believe in the efficacy of work, some overseers provided 'task work'. This included spade-labour on cultivated land or letting land free of rent in return for half the produce. In desperation they hired some paupers to collect stones from arable land, and others to throw the stones back so as to guarantee employment the next day. The result of the more degrading methods of helping the distressed and unemployed was the abandonment of any uniform system and a return to the widespread diversity that had prevailed since 1601. A third of the parishes investigated in 1833 had ceased to operate the Speenhamland system, but at Linton an allowance of 1s. above the normal county scale gave undesirable encouragement, it was said 'to the best fed and most comfortable and thriving population of paupers in the County of Cambridge'.[75] Those who disagreed with those sentiments were more likely to insist on the essential truth of Dr. Johnson's aphorism: 'a decent provision for the poor is the true test of a civilisation'.

❦ 6 ❦
The New Poor Law

By 1830 most of the middle and upper classes, accepting that some reform of the Poor Laws was imperative, severely criticised the alleged evil consequences of the allowance system. However, if the laws were abolished, what should the alternative be? The 'Captain Swing' riots of 1830 exacerbated the fears of landowners, farmers and magistrates. Lord Grey's Whig government, having crushed the revolt with un-

ashamed severity, appointed a Royal Commission to make a full investigation into the operation of the Poor Laws. The Report was to become a
classic document of English social policy and engendered a passionate
sense of injustice and hostility from the labouring classes of England. [76]

Charles Blomfield, the Tory Bishop of London, presided over the
Commission of nine. But the member who made the most impact was
Edwin Chadwick, a prodigious worker and ardent Utilitarian. There was
no representative of the working-class or the poor. The Commissioners,
firmly believing the new dogma of self-help, were inimical to what they
regarded as the laxity and immorality of workhouse life and the over-
liberal provision of poor-relief. Twenty-six investigators visited about
3000 parishes throughout England and Wales to collect information for
the Commission. In truth, their minds were already made up and as
this was not much more than a sample survey they have been accused
of being impressionistic, biased and selective in their findings. [77]

The remedies adopted by the Commission were simple and drastic
but were passed by Parliament in 1834 without significant oppositon.
The allowance system was to be abolished and with it all outdoor-relief
for the able-bodied and their families. These would be helped only if
they entered the workhouse and remained there. Application for relief
was now to be the real test of poverty. Meanwhile, in order to encourage
the agricultural labourer to find work, conditons in the new workhouses
were to be made less favourable (or 'less eligible') than those of the
lowest independent labourer: the theory being that if idleness were
made more unpleasant than work, people would find work. With the
horrors of mixed workhouses in mind the Commissioner also advised
segregation in separate workhouses according to age and sex. In order
to accomplish these changes the New Poor Law took power away from
the 15,000 existing parishes and set up 643 new Poor Law Unions, each
with its own workhouse. Within these Unions, the poor would be supervised by Boards of Guardians elected by the ratepayers. A Central Poor
Law Department was also established, with powers to issue orders and
regulations. But it was not responsible to Parliament, a freedom
regarded with great suspicion in the localities. It could be argued that
the real revolution occurred on the administrative side. Inspectors
were appointed to supervise and report on the introduction and operation of the new centralised system. [78]

It will be clear that the object of the new system was to discourage
pauperism, not to eradicate poverty. Chadwick hoped that this new
system would intimidate the undeserving poor, restore the principle of
work and independence, encourage fair wages, give the labourer

George Pryme and Thomas Spring-Rice, Whig M.P.s for the Borough of Cambridge in the 1830s.

employment and restore his lost sense of pride. He disapproved of the allowance system just as those in our own day who claim that 'free handouts', undermining the will to work, inevitably makes men soft. Hunger, Chadwick believed, made men industrious. The inference was that most pauperism was wilful and that the new Poor Law would, it was hoped, become a powerful stimulus to self-help. In the Commission's opinion society was doing the pauper a favour: being cruel to be kind.

Fear of the workhouse would produce employment. Strangely enough, this kind of reasoning was based on the assumption that enough work existed for everybody, an assumption that was to be brutally exposed as fallacious in the decade that followed.

What were the repercussions of the Act in Cambridgeshire? Conditions after the 'Swing riots' did not improve. Population and unemployment had continued to rise. Total expenditure on poor-relief in the county grew from £26,000 in 1783 to £103,000 by 1832. In 1834 Bourn had 130 farm labourers but work for only 100. Parish expenditure on relief had risen from £90 to £400 per annum. In Barrington fifty-four people were on permanent relief. In Orwell and Haslingfield the number was rarely less than fifty. Similar figures could be given for most villages in the county. Despite the findings of the Commission, it was not over-generosity but low wages and underemployment that had resulted in the expansion of the outdoor allowance system in Cambridgeshire. [79]

Until very recently it was believed that the New Poor Law was peacefully accepted in the Speenhamland counties of the South and East and violently resisted in the industrial North. However, the new law was strongly challenged in Cambridgeshire. [80] Admittedly, this resistance was rather narrowly based, uncoordinated and ultimately no more successful than elsewhere. But it was significant as a working-class response; and it indicated the strength of provincialism and the continuing belief in the superiority of localism as opposed to centralisation.

In general the middle classes in town and county, represented in the 1830s by their newly elected Whig M.P.s for the borough, George Pryme and Thomas Spring-Rice, welcomed the Act. In the words of one: 'We are not content to be now and forevermore the sturdy keepers of a degraded and immoral race of beings who draw their first breath and heave their last sigh within the walls of the poorhouse'. Such people were encouraged by the substantial drop in Poor Law rates that followed the introduction of the Act (the reduction was almost 50% by 1838). Not unnaturally this was a powerful inducement for acceptance among the town and county middle classes. [81]

On the other hand many of the greater Tory landowners in the county were shocked by the callous provisions of the new Act. It clashed with their own paternalistic outlook, an outlook that favoured the traditional and more deferential rural society, whose human values had already been so severely strained by enclosures, evictions, and the agrarian improvements, that in the more economically progressive counties many landowners had abdicated their social responsibilities. [82] The enclosure movement came late to Cambridgeshire. Its hardships, combined with the apparent inhumanity of the Act, created an unbridge-able gulf between landowners and labourers. The county magistracy, which had administered the old system, unhesitatingly rejected the new one, as did county doctors and churchmen. The doctors had profited under the old regime and lost contracts and income after 1834 while the county churchmen rejected it on humanitarian grounds. (Over half the membership of the Board of Guardians of the Peterborough Union were clergymen). [83] They all resented the centralising principles of the Act which deprived them of power and put it in the hands of the 'triple Autocrats of Somerset House' in London who were free of even minimal parliamentary accountability. [84] Predictably, much of their opposition was confined to writing letters to the press, boycotting elections for Boards of Guardians and meetings of the new Unions. [85] Having only recently recovered from the shock and turmoil of the 'Swing riots', they were unwilling to provoke further rebellion among the discontented labourers. [86]

It was, after all, the agricultural labourer who was faced with the full rigours of the Act, which presented him with the choice of starvation on the one hand or the break-up of his family and life in the new bastilles on the other. To him, it now appeared that to be poor was a crime. The Poor Law Commissioners, far removed from the localities, seemed like an alien power unmoved by pity, supplication or injustice. Life in the new workhouse was believed to be harsh and brutal, with every form of cruelty inflicted on the unfortunate inmate. Some of these beliefs appeared to be justified. [87] The pauper who left the workhouse forfeited all claims to poor-relief. The work was often of the most unpleasant or degrading kind, such as bone-crushing or oakum picking. The sexes were rigorously separated and families broken up. Until 1842 silence had to be observed at meals. The standards set in the workhouses were designed to be deterrent but the houses remained mixed and so the deserving and undeserving poor were forced to suffer equally. It is not surprising that people dreaded the possibility of ending their days in a workhouse or were appalled at the prospect of being buried in a pauper's grave. To be poor was an affliction; to be punished for it, infamy.

Recent historians, looking for mitigating factors, have concluded that in many ways paupers were better treated under the new Law. [88] Unions, it is argued, were newly built, had a medical officer attached, and were obliged to provide some education for workhouse children. And the Commissioners were not insensitive to criticism: what scandals there were, were usually the fault of local officials. At least one workhouse master in Cambridge was sacked for negligence; another alleged scandal reported in *The Times* was shown by Assistant Commissioner Wade to be completely without foundation. [89] Although accepting that many of the workhouses were clean and purpose-built, and that the diet was usually reasonable, we must concede that psychological hardship was intended and the order of the Commissioners was to make conditions 'less eligible'. In the words of Edwin Chadwick, Secretary to the Commissioners, this meant 'having all relief through the workhouse, making the workhouse an uninviting place of wholesome restraint, preventing any of its inmates from going out or receiving visitors without a written order to that effect from one of the overseers; disallowing beer and tobacco, and finding them work according to their ability; thus making the parish fund the last resource of a pauper and rendering the person who administers the relief the hardest taskmaster and the worst paymaster, that the idle and dissolute can apply to'. [90]

The appearance of Union Relieving Officers in the rural areas often provoked violence and rioting, as for example, near Royston in 1835 where one official was severely assaulted by a mob among which were many women, who were the chief sufferers under the Old and New Poor Law. Four women had already been imprisoned for a previous Poor Law disturbance at Bassingbourn in December 1831. [91] At Whitton the crowds threatening incendiarism told the overseers: 'You are starving the poor as fast as you can'. There were similar threats at Wisbech and at Ampthill in Bedfordshire. Here the mob made its intentions clear to the Relieving Officers. They said if the old allowance system were discontinued 'we'll have the money out of your pockets and the blood out of your veins'. [92]

The greatest stimulus to social action was the building of the new Union workhouses in the towns and counties of England. These oppressive buildings symbolised the major threat to the freedom and independence of the poor. Predictably, the poor reacted. The building of Linton workhouse had to be postponed because the newly-elected Guardians feared that it might be burnt down. When erected, it was attacked and all the windows were smashed. At nearby Saffron Walden and Bishop's Stortford both workhouses were burnt to the ground in December 1835. Such attacks were not common in Cambridgeshire between 1834 and 1836 because local resistance was disorganised, sporadic and leaderless. Faced with the determination of the Poor Law Guardians, the poor failed to prevent the implementation of the Act.

In 1836 a leader did finally emerge in the county. He was the Rev. F. H. Maberly, Vicar of Kingston, a well-known local agitator and

Workhouse plan by architect Thomas Nash, 1836.

eccentric. [93] In 1818 he had publicly condemned the decline in morals among University undergraduates [94] and in the following decade he doggedly opposed the granting of Catholic Emancipation. He even threatened to impeach the King in 1823, and the Prime Minister, the Duke of Wellington in 1828, if it were passed. [95] In the middle 'thirties Maberly's attack on the Poor Law gave him an important place in the national history of the anti-Poor Law movement. [96] His main appeal was to the county agricultural labourers. In his pamphlet *To the Poor and their friends...* he condemned the cessation of outdoor-relief and the evils of the workhouse. The Act, he claimed, was 'tyrannical, unconstitutional, anti-scriptural, anti-Christian, unnatural, cruel and impolitic in the extreme'.[97] It encouraged homosexuality by segregating the sexes and promiscuity by redefining the bastardy laws in favour of fathers; it was an abdication of responsibility by the ruling orders which would divide society and provoke rebellion among the labouring poor. However, he rejected the suggestion that his agitation was political: 'I agitate to benefit the poor...to preserve privileges, not to destroy them'. [98]

He denied any intention of leading a labourers' revolt: his opposition was to be responsible and constitutional, using press, platform and pulpit to achieve the repeal of the hated Act. He certainly wished his campaign to be seen as part of the national anti-Poor Law movement, which was particularly strong in the North of England. He attended national meetings in London and became a friend of Richard Oastler, renowned for his vigorous leadership of the northern movement. In fact, Maberly's movement had much in common with its northern counterpart: the exaggerated rhetoric of the pamphlet, the stimulating oratory of the public meeting, and the petition in an effort to promote constitutional change. In his agitation he used pamphlets, newspaper letters and handbills but his main emphasis was on outdoor meetings organised to ensure maximum public support. He tried to invest these meetings with a sense of occasion and usually arrived in a decorated cart, preceded by colourfully dressed cheer-leaders and accompanied by fiddlers, pipers and dancers. Banners, placards and flags were displayed during the speeches as Maberly, and his two 'reverend accomplices' Clack and Lund, denounced the Poor Law and the degraded condition of the labourers of the county. Petitions were circulated for signatures; at the end of the meeting the leaders and labourers would repair to the nearest public house to quench their thirst and continue their discussions. [99]

Maberly began his campaign with a meeting at Bourn in the summer of 1836. By this date most of the Cambridgeshire Unions had already been organised and the first workhouses were under construction. Meetings at Cambridge, and adjacent to the unfinished workhouse near Royston, followed. The Home Secretary, Lord John Russell, had already warned Maberly that he would be held personally responsible for any breach of the peace that occurred at his gatherings, but Maberly refused to be intimidated. [100] The Royston Poor Law Guardians, fearing an attack on the workhouse, arranged for a body of Metropolitan Police to be sent to Royston to maintain order. Fears and expectations ran high and when the labourers arrived it was clear that they thought Maberly was going to lead them in the destruction of the workhouse. Disappointed at the orderliness of the proceedings, drenched by a heavy rain, and receiving, they complained, 'no information which instructed, interested or gratified them', they left the meeting determined to attend no more like it. [101]

Pressure on Maberly mounted in an effort to get him to call off his campaign. The Lord Lieutenant of the County, the Earl of Hardwicke, and Maberly's superior, the Bishop of Ely, warned him of the consequences of his actions, but meetings followed at Huntingdon on July 7, Ely and Littleport on July 9, Saffron Walden July 16, St. Neots

July 21 and St. Ives on July 25. [102] All these meetings received good coverage in the local press where there are further references to meetings held at Wisbech, Linton, Caxton and Bury St. Edmunds later in the year.

The national Anti-Poor Law movement renewed its activities in the spring of 1837. As enthusiasm revived, Maberly called the first meeting of the 1837 campaign in Cambridge. [103] Further meetings were organised at Huntingdon and St. Neots. A petition signed by Maberly, allegedly expressing the wishes of 35,000 people, was presented to the House of Lords. [104] They were extremely unsympathetic and derisively rejected it. Maberly, short of money and under ever-increasing pressures, decided to suspend the calling of public meetings where support and encouragement could now at best be described as only moderate. [105] In the summer he made one final attempt to put his case against the Poor Law at the Cambridge borough election nomination, but was promptly arrested by the newly-formed Cambridge town police. However, an irate public 'rescued' him from the town gaol and carried him back, shoulder-high, to Parker's Piece, where he defiantly finished his speech. [106]

Disappointed at the lack of interest generated by his campaign, but convinced of the rightness of his cause, Maberly continued to defend individual labourers against the oppressions of the Poor Law and, with fervour undiminished, even attempted a break-in at Caxton workhouse to rescue a pauper he believed to be unjustly committed. Clearly the campaign had failed. In November 1837 Assistant Commissioner Wade, in a report to the Poor Law Commissioners, was able to declare 'that in no part of this district is there any manifestation of discontent, either existing or anticipated'. [107]

Why did Maberly's campaign in Cambridgeshire fail? The earlier propaganda campaign organised against the evils of the Old Poor Law convinced most people of the necessity for some reform, and the prospect of a reduction in the soaring poor-rates was especially attractive to the middle classes. On the other hand, the peculiar geographical and economic divisions of the county, the poor communications network and the traditional subservience of the agricultural labourers (even in times of acute distress) made it extremely difficult to organise a unified opposition and mount an early challenge to the introduction to the Act. The latter was doubly difficult because in the period up to 1837 there was little or no visual evidence of the new system until the first workhouses were constructed. Some parishes, such as St. Andrew the Less in Cambridge, opposed the principle of centralisation from the start and at

Caxton Workhouse and Gibbet.

first refused to elect Poor Law Guardians to run the new system. [108] Chesterton and Linton Unions, once set up, refused to terminate outdoor-relief. By 1837 such uncoordinated and isolated responses were easily overcome. Opposition, even under Maberly, was not united and was organised too late to be effective.

The sympathy of some landowners, humanitarians, clerics and radicals was of little practical value. At root what the movement lacked was the drive and organising ability of the town and county middle classes. Though Maberly stressed the constitutional and non-revolutionary aims of his campaign, the propertied classes were unwilling to be associated with a movement that appeared to encourage violence. In short, Maberly failed to convince the ratepayers. Equally the agricultural labourers, placated by two years of good harvests and employment in 1835 and 1836, were unable to see the relevance of petitions to Parliament while workhouses were being built in their parishes. Maberly, never able to rely on the wholehearted, enthusiastic support of any one class, thus got the worst of every possible world.

It could be argued, however, that his was not the only failure. In many ways the Commissioners also failed. The Act was never fully introduced into the industrial Midlands and the North, where many Guardians flatly refused to implement the workhouse test. Furthermore, the new regulations did not reduce the cost of relief for very long. Wages did not rise and, by retaining the Act of Settlement, the government discouraged migration from the over-populated countryside to the industrialised town. The vital question of finance and Poor Law rating was also left untouched. Finally, although the Act may have had some success in deterring pauperism, it failed hopelessly to deal with the problem of poverty. As the Victorian age proceeded, the genuine poor had to be provided for by other legislative and administrative measures more humane than the 1834 Act. Paradoxically, the State in the end had to provide an alternative to the Poor Law—and in doing so laid the foundations of the modern welfare state.

❦ 7 ❦
The End of the Poor Law

In 1847 the Poor Law Commission, which had existed since 1834, gave way to a Poor Law Board which in turn lasted until 1871. It was then replaced by the Local Government Board, not because of any development in Poor Law policy, but because of an administrative merger of Poor Law, Public Health and Local Government.

During the years of Maberly's campaign the parishes of Cambridgeshire were formed into nine Unions: Cambridge, Chesterton, Caxton and Arrington, Ely, Linton, Newmarket, North Witchford, Whittlesey, and Wisbech. Most of these Unions encroached territorially on other counties; for example Newmarket Union was partly in Suffolk, Royston partly in Hertfordshire, Wisbech partly in Norfolk. Cambridge Union attempted the separation of the children and of the aged and impotent poor from the able-bodied but the policy was soon abandoned: a new, general, mixed workhouse was built in Mill Road in 1838. Hobson's workhouse was closed in 1837. For many years it had been used by the University authorities for the confinement of 'common women'. Even at this late date the unfortunate ladies were often whipped. C. H. Cooper records from the Treasurer's Accounts 'Paid Homer Johnson by order of Mr. Vice-Chancellor for whipping ten women 10s.'. [109] Separate classification was not a viable proposition for the poorer rural unions. A new workhouse was built at Ely in 1837 and later at Wisbech where, true to its progressive and enlightened tradition, it was designed to look like a large Elizabethan dwelling. The Poor Law Commission investigators in 1834 grudgingly admitted that the former workhouse had not been 'ill-regulated'. Under the supervision of the chairman of the Poor Law Board, the Rev. H. Fardell, it pursued a costly but exceptionally humane and understanding policy in its attitude to the resident poor. [110]

The new Poor Law did not cure poverty. Most of the working classes of town and county were still likely to experience it at some time in their lives and would be forced to rely on the help of family, friends and occasional credit in order to survive. This kind of recurrent poverty was believed to be inevitable and was taken for granted. The Victorians regarded poverty as a social fact. It was pauperism that the government continued to worry about. The Commissioners in 1834 did not investigate the causes or nature of poverty. They were concerned primarily with pauperism, the allowance system and rural unemployment. As it happened the problem in the century after 1834 turned out to be urban, industrial poverty, for which the new Poor Law was totally ill-adapted and in 1850 the *Cambridge Chronicle* was still appalled by the disgraceful, dirty and degrading conditions suffered by the poor of Cambridge and Ely. [111]

What was the major cause of poverty during this later period? The most obvious was low wages; another the large family. Sickness, particularly when it struck down the breadwinner, was another cause and if death occurred the widow and dependent children were bound to suffer. Old age completed the cycle. Surprisingly, these facts had to be 'discovered'. [112] In Cambridgeshire almost twenty per cent of outdoor relief was due to sickness and more than half the paupers in county workhouses were over sixty years of age. [113] The Victorian middle classes believed that the poor became poverty-stricken through intemperance and indolence. It needed the dedicated investigations and writings of such men as Henry Mayhew, Charles Booth and Seebohm Rowntree to expose the true nature of late Victorian urban poverty. The results of their pioneering social work shocked the conscience of the nation and challenged the long-held belief in the efficacy of individualism and *laissez-faire*. They made many people far more critical of the existing Poor Law system and also of the voluntary organisations for the relief of poverty that developed in mid-century. [114]

One of the most important of these was the Charity Organisation Society (C.O.S.), founded in 1869. A Cambridge branch was organised a decade later and its president, Dr. H. Sidgwick, persuaded the old Mendicity Society to close Mendicity House at Barnwell and integrate with the newly founded organisation. The C.O.S. was rate-aided but relied mainly on voluntary donations. In the 1880s it built eighteen cottages for the poor in Gloucester Street. At first sight, the C.O.S. appeared to reflect all that was callous and inhuman in the new Poor Law. It opposed State aid and indiscriminate almsgiving; investigated fraudulent charities and discouraged the unwarranted intrusion of untrained middle class 'do-gooders' into the lives of the poor. Discriminating aid to help the poor regain their independence was the

Dolebread distributed at a funeral in 1864, from G.N. Maynard, *Illustrations of Whittlesford.* Vol. IX (n.d but 1890), p. 197.

Society's aim, but its main contribution was its insistence on investigation to determine facts on which sound decisions could be made. [115]
An alternative approach was adopted by the Salvation Army, which concerned itself more with the symptoms than the causes of poverty. The Army was not very popular; the Cambridge newspapers of the 1880s contain many stories of assault on members (and on their musical instruments) during marches through the town.

In spite of the growth of voluntary organisations such as the C.O.S, the public system instituted in 1834 continued as before with the emphasis on keeping down costs, and therefore Poor Law rates. Outdoor relief, still cheap, was continued for the able-bodied. As a result, the new workhouses were soon filled with the sick, aged, orphaned and mentally defective. In rural areas the workhouses became reservoirs of unemployed surplus labour in winter months and a kind of labour exchange in spring and harvest time. Many farmers favoured such a system as it kept available a pool of labour which they could draw on according to need. [116] Conditions in workhouses still caused concern: a popular belief was that Boards of Guardians guarded the rates more than the interests of the poor. Rates, especially in the poorer parishes where the need was always greatest, continued to be extremely difficult to collect. In the 1880s this led to something like a crusade, backed by the Cambridge Ratepayers' Association, against the granting of alleged indiscriminate out-relief to the poor. [117] One of the major faults of the new Poor Law was that it ignored financial factors. In 1865 the county unions adopted the system of levying a uniform rate on the whole union. The town of Cambridge had anticipated this reform in 1856.

Within the workhouses, attempts were made to organise help according to needs. Pauper schools were set up for the young, pauper infirmaries for the sick, with separate wards for the mentally defective. Treatment of the able-bodied remained problematic; it was often either impossible (as in times of high unemployment) or unwise to enforce the workhouse test in spite of the proddings of the newly established Local Government Board. It was clear that the Act of 1834 was not fulfilling administrative expectations. The system instituted in 1834 never developed for two very good reasons. Firstly, the working classes feared and hated it; secondly, they resisted having anything to do with any of its provisions because of the stigma attached. Pauperism had become a status that affected a person's whole life. Any person thus categorised became a pauper for all purposes and involved his family as well. Paupers became a distinct group of second-class citizens with restricted rights. The building of Poor Law infirmaries and schools confirmed this shameful status. By the late nineteenth century, therefore, it was becoming increasingly irrelevant as the state tackled the problems of pauperism separately. For example, the new school boards set up in 1870 dealt with child poverty through school meals and medical inspection. Schemes for old age pensions were also being discussed during these years. [118] Differences of opinion over what to do with the able-bodied poor led to the appointment in 1905 of the Royal Commission on the Poor Laws. Meanwhile, voluntary organisations such as the Salvation Army had to develop their own methods of dealing with the vagrant and destitute. [119]

The 1905 Commission included C. S. Loch, Octavia Hill, Charles Booth and Beatrice Webb. It discovered that 14,000 children under sixteen were still housed in mixed, general workhouses; that lunatics, idiots and imbeciles mixed freely with other inmates and that infants, children, pregnant women, the sick and the aged were looked after by fellow-paupers. Thirty per cent of the inmates were ill and within the system remained virtually uncared-for. There was no separate accommodation for the insane. Despite finding some general improvements, the Commissioners were appalled by some of the conditions they had witnessed. [120] The Report gives some interesting figures for Cambridgeshire. There were almost 11,000 paupers in the county (32 per cent men, 42 per cent women and 26 per cent children), slightly above the national average of 5 per cent. About two-thirds were in permanent need of help; pauperism was highest in the rural unions. More women than men received outdoor relief but men predominated in the workhouses. The average number of children per workhouse was twenty three, but many others were boarded out or maintained in voluntary preventative, or training homes in Cambridge, such as the Hills Road Training Home for Girls and the Harvey Goodwin Home for Boys. [121]

Though the 1905 Commission condemned the system of poor-relief, it failed to produce a united Report and so nothing was done before 1914. In the meantime poverty was receiving help from a different source. The Liberal Party, through its own programme of social reforms, which sought to provide special services for distinct groups outside the Poor Law, was making an important contribution to poor-relief. These reforms included free school meals and regular medical inspections, old age pensions, and unemployment insurance and labour exchanges for the unemployed. In Cambridge, Barnwell and Romsey Town, the 'industrial' and manufacturing areas still housed enormous numbers of poor, whom Eglantine Jebb described as 'pitiful caricatures of men and women, poor puny wastrels, starvelings, degenerates, on whose faces the dull suffering of hopelessness has left its indelible stamp'. Although the numbers in receipt of poor-relief fell, and there was much discussion about 'the breaking up of the Poor Law' and the humanizing of its administration, poverty (as the researches of A. L. Bowley and B. Seebohm Rowntree revealed) was still extensive in the years before World War I. [122]

The campaign for the break-up of the Poor Laws continued between the Wars. The dole was introduced as a protection for the unemployed against destitution. Meanwhile, responsibilities of the Poor Law authorities were being transferred to other agencies such as health, education, welfare and employment. In Cambridgeshire the total number of those in receipt of poor-relief had fallen to about half the 1907 figure by 1930. In 1929 the Boards of Guardians were abolished and

Whittlesford Gildhall, formerly used as a poorhouse.

their powers handed over to Public Assistance Committees. [123] The Poor Law was not abolished (the mixed workhouse survived) but placed under new management with a view to its eventual disappearance. The task of Public Assistance was 'to provide such relief as may be necessary for the lame, impotent, old, blind and such other persons as are poor and unable to work'. [124] However, they were to enforce a strict means test which provoked resentment and humiliation and, like the workhouse before it, was destined to leave an ineradicable mark on popular culture in the Thirties. The 1930 Poor Law Act abolished the workhouse test and the term 'pauper'.

Since 1930, the workhouses and casual wards of the county have been coordinated and gradually reduced in number under the schemes of their respective County Councils. The three remaining wards in the Isle of Ely, at Ely, Doddington and Wisbech, were closed, and a new ward built at Guyhirn, which is on the popular tramping route between Great Yarmouth and Birmingham. Outside the Isle the only institutions retained by 1938 were those at Cambridge and Chesterton. The latter, now known as Union Lane, was used primarily for 'casuals'. These were supervised by the East Anglian Joint Vagrancy Committee, of which Cambridge was a constituent member. The aim was to direct casuals to large urban centres where they might find employment and thereby be encouraged to give up aimless wandering. Those over 65 years of age were to be housed in Public Assistance institutions and the young put in hostels and apprenticed. [125] Itinerants and gypsies were ignored. Cambridgeshire and other counties inevitably saw them as being outside the system and moved them on as quickly as decency allowed.

In 1942 the Beveridge Report proposed the introduction of a wide scheme of social welfare which proclaimed the end of the Poor Law. According to Sir William Beveridge, man required five Freedoms: Freedom from Want, Disease, Ignorance, Squalor and Idleness. His Report included plans for social security, a health service, family allowances, education and housing. The responsibility of the state for the welfare of its citizen was recognised more explicitly than ever before and the term Welfare State was born. With the passing of the National Assistance Act in 1948 the Poor Law was finally abolished. [126] The N.A.B. was charged with the duty of relieving anybody whose resources did not match their requirements. With some satisfaction Ernest Bevin was able to announce: "At last we have buried the Poor Law". [127]

❧ 8 ❧
Conclusion

The Poor Law may have been buried, but this did not mean an end to poverty. Poverty is, of course, a relative term. Being poor in India and being poor in England can be vastly different. To be poor means to be deprived of the basic necessities of life but one can argue about what constitutes 'the basic necessities' from society to society and from generation to generation. Certainly there is a comparative element: it is much more difficult to be poor amidst plenty than amidst destitution.

In the last thirty years the working classes of Cambridgeshire, helped by the National Health Service, pensions, family allowances and other social services are better off than ever. And yet the problem of poverty persists. In mid-Anglia, still one of the lowest wage areas in England, local Poverty Action Groups continue to draw our attention to child poverty, low-income families and inadequate housing. Claimants' Unions emphasise the ignorance of the poor concerning their welfare rights. Organisations such as Age Concern publicise the plight of the old in an age of inflation. Vagrants, tramps and gypsies continue to be a source of irritation to many who have dealings with them.

Local newspapers ensure that urban poverty is highlighted and therefore, to a certain extent, alleviated. Rural poverty, though less obvious, equally needs our attention and lacks any effective social or political representation. We no longer believe that such a state of affairs should exist. Yet there is a danger that we may fall back on the Victorian attitude of accepting poverty as a social fact and blaming it on individual weakness. Worst of all, we may abdicate our sense of social responsibility altogether and leave the problem to the welfare state. In the struggle to end poverty, County Councils have the power but not always the will; voluntary organisations have the will, but not always the power; so the poor are still with us.

Notes and References

1. C.H. Cooper, *Annals of Cambridge*, II, (Cambridge, 1843), p. 332.
2. *Victoria County History, Cambridgeshire and the Isle of Ely*, II (London, 1948), p.90.
3. J.C. Cox, *Cambridgeshire* (London, 1914), pp. 21-22. See also W.E. Tate, *The parish chest* (Cambridge, 1946), p. 189.
4. T.D. Atkinson, *Cambridge described and illustrated* (London, 1897), pp. 15,58. See also T.D. Atkinson, 'Gilds of Cambridge' in *Cambridge Antiquarian Society* [*C.A.S.*] IX, 1897.
5. F.J. Gardiner, *History of Wisbech* (Wisbech, 1898), pp. 87-90; *V.C.H. Cambs.*, IV (1953), pp. 255-56.
6. See J.J. Jusserand, *English wayfaring life in the Middle Ages* (London, 1889; repr. 1970).
7. E.M. Hampson, *The treatment of poverty in Cambridgeshire* (Cambridge, 1934), p. 4.
8. See G. Salgado, *The Elizabethan underworld* (London, 1977).
9. J.W.E. Conybeare, *A history of Cambridgeshire* (London, 1897), pp. 188-92; J. Pound, *Poverty and vagrancy in Tudor England* (London, 1971), pp. 3-23.
10. Pound, *Poverty in Tudor England*, pp. 39-43.
11. Cooper, *Annals*, I, p. 385.
12. See E. Christian, *Charges delivered to Grand Juries in the Isle of Ely upon vagrants etc.* (London, 1819), p.398.
13. See J. Pound, 'An Elizabethan census of the poor', in *Birmingham University Historical Journal*, 1962.
14. Cooper, *Annals*, II, pp. 109-110.

15. Pound, *Poverty in Tudor England,* pp. 47-48.
16. *V.C.H. Cambs.,* II, p. 93; IV, pp. 260-61.
17. See *Linton Vestry Records* 1577-1601.
18. A. Gray, *The town of Cambridge* (Cambridge, 1925), pp. 91-98.
19. See W.K. Jordan, *Philanthropy in England 1480-1660* (London, 1959).
20. See E.M. Leonard, *Early history of English poor relief* (London, 1900).
21. H.P. Stokes, 'Cambridge parish workhouses', in *C.A.S.,* XV, 1911, p. 80.
22. Leonard, *English poor relief,* p. vii.
23. C. Wilson, *England's apprenticeship* (London, 1965), pp. XI-XII.
24. Leonard, *English poor relief,* pp. 165-183.
25. J.E. Foster (ed.), *Churchwardens' Accounts of St. Mary the Great,* 1504-1635 (Cambridge, 1905), *Item* 372 b, p. 442.
26. Cooper, *Annals,* III, pp. 222-30; Stokes, 'Cambridge workhouses', *C.A.S.,* Ch. III.
27. See *Great St. Mary's MS. Vestry Book* for the years 1642-46; A. Kingston, *East Anglia and the Great Civil War* (London, 1897), pp. 43, 89; C. Holmes, *The Eastern Association in the English Civil War* (Cambridge, 1974), pp. 54-55.
28. G. Taylor, *The problem of poverty, 1660-1834* (London, 1969), pp. 56-66.
29. S.J.D. Mitchell, *A history of the Perse School, 1615-1976* (Cambridge, 1976), pp. 5-13; Hampson, *Treatment of poverty,* pp. 28-30; *V.C.H. Cambs.,* IV, p. 43.
30. *MS. Corporation Minute and Order Book, Wisbech.* Quoted by Hampson, *op. cit.,* p. 39 and Ch. III.
31. *Linton Vestry Records,* 1618.
32. *MS. Overseers' Accounts, Littleport;* Hampson, *op. cit.,* pp. 43-44.
33. For a good account see E. Lipson, *The economic history of England,* III, (4th edn., London, 1947), pp. 457-69, 533-35.
34. Hampson, *Treatment of poverty,* pp. 52-53.
35. *V.C.H. Cambs.,* II, p. 102, n. 44.
36. Stokes, 'Parish workhouses', *C.A.S.,* XV, p. 84.
37. See Christian, *Charges to Grand Juries,* Ch. VI.
38. *MS. Quarter Sessions Reports,* 1704-8; Hampson, *op. cit.,* pp. 129-30.
39. Hampson, *Treatment of poverty,* pp. 134-36.
40. *Ibid.,* p. 139.
41. See W.M. Palmer, *Meldreth Parish Records,* 1896.
42. *Q.S. Minute and Order Books* 1660-1831. Quoted by Hampson, *op. cit.,* p. 167.
43. Hampson, *Treatment of poverty,* p. 176.
44. Hampson, *op. cit.,* Ch. V; Taylor, *Problem of poverty,* pp. 30-33, 50-53.
45. S. and B. Webb, *English poor law history,* Part I (London, 1926 *repr.* 1963), p. 212.
46. Gardiner, *Wisbech,* pp. 43, 312; Watson, *Wisbech,* p. 315.
47. *Great St. Mary's MS. Vestry Book,* 1734; *Hampson* op. cit., p. 83.
48. Stokes, 'Parish workhouses', *C.A.S.* XV, Appendix II, pp. 134-137.
49. Stokes, *loc. cit.,* p. 109.
50. J. Micklebourgh, *The great duty of labour and work* (Cambridge, 1751), pp. 20-21.
51. Hampson, *op. cit.,* p. 87.
52. H. Gunning, *Reminiscences of the University, Town and County of Cambridge,* I, (London, 1854), p. 173; Stokes, *loc. cit.,* pp. 110-112.
53. Hampson, *Treatment of poverty,* pp. 87-91.
54. T. Woolmer, *A beggar poet* (1887). Quoted by Hampson, *op. cit.,* p. 97
55. See Hampson, *op. cit.,* p. 100, Ch. VIII; Stokes, 'Parish workhouses', pp. 105-9.
56. See J.E. Foster (ed.), *The diary of S.N., alderman of Cambridge 1662-1717* (Cambridge, 1890) p. 10; Taylor, *Problem of poverty,* pp. 76-78.
57. For the background to economic and social change during these years see my: *Cambridge newspapers and opinion, 1780-1850* (Cambridge, 1977).
58. See J.D. Chambers and G.E. Mingay, *The agricultural revolution 1750-1880* (London, 1966); D. Marshall, *The English poor in the eighteenth century* (London, 1926).
59. J.D. Marshall, *The old Poor Law* (London, 1968), pp. 26-27.

60. Hampson, *op. cit.*, p. 106.
61. *V.C.H. Cambs.*, V, (London, 1973), pp. 234-35.
62. Hampson, *op. cit.*, pp. 187-88, Ch. XV. For a more detailed investigation see *Poor Law Commission Report 1834*, Appendix A, pt. I.
63. Cooper, *Annals*, IV, p. 454; *Cambridge Chronicle*, January-July 1795.
64. *Cambridge Chronicle*, 25 Feb. 1797, 16 Nov. 1799, 22 Nov. 1800.
65. Marshall, *Old Poor Law*, pp., 12-15, 19-20.
66. *MS. Vestry Books Sawston, Bottisham*, 1792-94.
67. Hampson, *op. cit.*, pp. 194-95.
68. But see Marshall, *Old Poor Law*, pp. 43-46.
69. J. Denson, *A peasant's voice to landowners* (Cambridge, 1830), p. 46.
70. *Cambridge Chronicle*, 7 Nov. 1807.
71. *Ibid.*, 22 Jan., 4 May 1819; Cooper, *Annals*, IV, pp. 517-18.
72. See E.J. Hobsbawm and G. Rudé, *Captain Swing* (London, 1969).
73. *MS. Quarter Sessions Reports*, Cambs. (Bassingbourn, Oct. 1821).
74. *V.C.H. Cambs.*, II, pp. 102-3. See also Christian, *Charges delivered to Grand Juries* (1819).
75. Hampson, *op. cit.*, pp. 201, 203-19.
76. S.G. and E.O.A. Checkland (eds.), *The Poor Law Report of 1834* (Harmondsworth, 1974).
77. M. Blaug, 'The myth of the old Poor Law and the making of the new', *and* 'The Poor Law report re-examined', in *Journal of Economic History*, 1963, 1964.
78. Webbs, *English poor law history I*, (London, 1929), pp. 47-103. See also J.R. Poynter, *Society and pauperism, 1795-1834* (London, 1969).
79. *V.C.H. Cambs.*, V, pp. 11-12, 234-35.
80. See A.J. Peacock, 'Village radicalism in East Anglia', in J.P.D. Dunbabin (ed.), *Rural discontent in nineteenth century Britain* (London, 1974).
81. See *A letter about the Poor Laws to the electors of Cambridge...by a member of the University* (Cambridge, 1837).
82. See my: *Cambridge newspapers*, pp. 48, 58-9, 94-6.
83. See H.F. Tebbs, *Peterborough: a history* (Cambridge, 1978).
84. *Cambridge Chronicle*, 25 Aug. 1838; *Cambridge Independent Press*, 13 Feb., 26 Mar., 15 Oct. 1836, 25 Aug. 1838.
85. See D. Fraser (ed.), *The New Poor Law in the nineteenth century* (London, 1976), Ch. 5.
86. *Cambridge Independent Press*, 6 July 1839.
87. *Cambridge Chronicle*, 3,18,24 June 1836; 25 Mar. 1837; 29 June 1839.
88. D. Roberts, 'How cruel was the Victorian Poor Law?' and U. Henriques, 'How cruel was the Victorian Poor Law?' in *Historical Journal* VI, 1963; XI, 1968.
89. See *The Times*, 4 July 1837.
90. J.L. and B. Hammond, *The bleak age* (London, 1967) p. 114.
91. *MS. History of Congregationalism in Bassingbourn 1790-1878*, ff. 98-99.
92. *Cambridge Chronicle*, 16 Jan., 22 Aug. 1835; *Cambridge Independent Press*, 23 May 1835.
93. See S.E. Minnis, *A turbulent priest* (unpublished pamphlet, n.d. but 195-).
94. F.H. Maberly, *The melancholy and awful death of Lawrence Dundas* (London, 1818).
95. *Cambridge Chronicle*, 29 June 1829, 23 July, 20 Aug. 1830.
96. N. Edsall, *The Anti-Poor Law Movement 1834-44* (Manchester, 1971), pp. 41-3.
97. F.H. Maberly, *To the poor and their friends* (London, 1836), p. 11.
98. *Cambridge Chronicle*, 25 Nov. 1836.
99. *Cambridge Independent Press*, 4,16 July 1836, 29 April 1837.
100. Maberly, *To the poor*, p. 9.
101. *The Hertford Reformer*, 28 June 1836; A. Kingston, *History of Royston* (London, 1906), pp. 178-79; A. Kingston, *Fragments of two centuries* (Royston, 1893), pp. 171-72.

102. G. Wythen Baxter, *The book of the bastilles* (London, 1841), pp. 57-58.
103. *Cambridge Chronicle*, 8 April, 6 May 1837.
104. See Maberly, *To the poor*, Appendix.
105. See *The Times*, 16th July 1837.
106. *Cambridge Chronicle*, 29 July 1837.
107. R.J. Hite, 'Reaction to the Poor Law amendment act in Cambridgeshire'. (*unpublished B.A. Dissertation*, University of York, 1975), p.30.
108. *Cambridge Independent Press*, 26 Mar. 1836.
109. Cooper, *Annals*, IV, p. 274 n.
110. Gardiner, *History of Wisbech*, pp. 312-15.
111. *Cambridge Chronicle*, 5 Oct. 1850.
112. M.E. Rose, *The relief of poverty, 1834-1914* (London, 1972), pp. 17-20.
113. See *Cambridge Union Minute Books*, 1834-1900.
114. Rose, *Relief of poverty*, pp. 20-24. See also B. Harrison, 'Philanthropy and the Victorians', in *Victorian Studies* IX, 1966.
115. E. Jebb, *Cambridge. A brief study in social questions* (Cambridge, 1906), Ch. XII; F.A. Keynes, *By-ways of Cambridge history* (Cambridge, 1947).
116. A. Digby, 'The labour market and the continuity of social policy after 1884' in *Economic History Review*, 28, 1975.
117. *Camb. Ind. Press*, June, July, August, 1883.
118. See H.V. Emy, *Liberals, radicals and social politics 1892-1914* (Cambridge, 1973).
119. See D. Owen, *English philanthropy 1660-1960* (Cambridge, Mass., 1965).
120. P. Gregg, *A social and economic history of Britain* (London, 1950), p. 492.
121. *V.C.H. Cambs.*, II, pp. 98-99.
122. See B.B. Gilbert, *The evolution of national insurance in Great Britain: the origins of the Welfare State* (London, 1966).
123. D.C. Morrison, *State and private aid* (Cambridge, 1922), Ch. II.
124. T.H. Marshall, *Social policy* (London, 1965), p. 117.
125. *V.C.H. Cambs.*, II, pp. 99-100.
126. D. Fraser, *The evolution of the British Welfare State* (London, 1973), Ch. 9.
127. Fraser, *op. cit.*, p. 213.

Bibliographical Note

There is an abundance of original source material available for Cambridgeshire. Parish Vestry Books, MS. collections, Churchwardens' Accounts, Corporation and Quarter Sessions Records, Charity Reports and Board of Guardians' Minute Books can all be consulted in the County Record Office and at Wisbech and Saffron Walden Museums. The Public Record Office holds Home Office Papers, Poor Law Commission and Poor Law Board Reports. A valuable guide to the use of such material is W. E. Tate, *The parish chest* (Cambridge, 1946). Contemporary newspapers, annals, pamphlets and tracts can provide a stimulating introduction to the topic and, though they must be treated with some caution, works of fiction and poetry such as those by Fielding, Goldsmith, Crabbe, Dickens and Orwell, can add to our understanding. The indispensable general work is the Webbs's *English poor law history* and, for the county, Hampson's *Treatment of poverty in Cambridgeshire.*